SHARKS!
STRANGE AND WONDERFUL

BY LAURENCE PRINGLE • **ILLUSTRATED BY MERYL HENDERSON**

*Port Jackson Shark—
up to 5^1/$_2$ feet long*

BOYDS MILLS PRESS
HONESDALE, PENNSYLVANIA

For Joshua Dailey, who loves books, and who may someday love sharks
—L.P.

To my dear friend Mary Anne Asciutto, who is also my wonderful agent—
thank you for helping me throughout my career
—M.H.

The author thanks Dr. Kim N. Holland of the Hawaii Institute of Marine Biology, University of Hawaii, for reviewing the text and illustrations of this book for accuracy.

Text copyright © 2001 by Laurence Pringle
Illustrations copyright © 2001 by Meryl Henderson

First paperback edition, 2008

Boyds Mills Press, Inc.
815 Church Street
Honesdale, Pennsylvania 18431
Printed in China

The Library of Congress has cataloged the hardcover edition as follows:

Pringle, Laurence.
Sharks! : strange and wonderful / by Laurence Pringle ; illustrated by
Meryl Henderson. —1st ed.
 [32]p. : col. ill. ; cm.
Summary: Dramatic, factual illustrations accompany facts about sharks.
ISBN 1-56397-863-6
1. Sharks. I. Henderson, Meryl, ill. II. Title.
597.3 21 2001 CIP AC
00-101643
Paperback ISBN 978-1-59078-571-3

The text of this book is set in 15-point Clearface Regular.
The illustrations were done in liquid acrylics.
10 9 8 7 6 5 4 3 2 1

Scalloped Hammerhead—
up to 15 feet long

Sharks are a special kind of fish. They can be small enough to fit in your hand, or bigger than a school bus.

Zebra Shark—
up to 11 feet long

Whale Shark—
up to 46 feet long

Goblin Shark—
up to 12 feet long

Angel Shark—
up to 5 feet long

Dwarf Shark—
up to 10 inches long

Megamouth Shark—
up to 17 feet long

Nearly four hundred types of sharks swim in the oceans. Each year new kinds of sharks are discovered. One strange-looking shark with a huge mouth—the megamouth—was first seen in 1976.

Sharks are relatives of other sea creatures called rays, skates, and sawfish.

Manta Ray—
up to 29 feet wide

Sawfish—
up to 21 feet long

Southern Stingrays—
up to 6 feet wide

Rough Skate—
up to 3 1/2 feet wide

Sharks are unusual in many ways. Most fish have a bony skeleton, but a shark does not have a bone in its body. Its skeleton is made of a strong material called *cartilage*. You can feel cartilage in your own ears and nose.

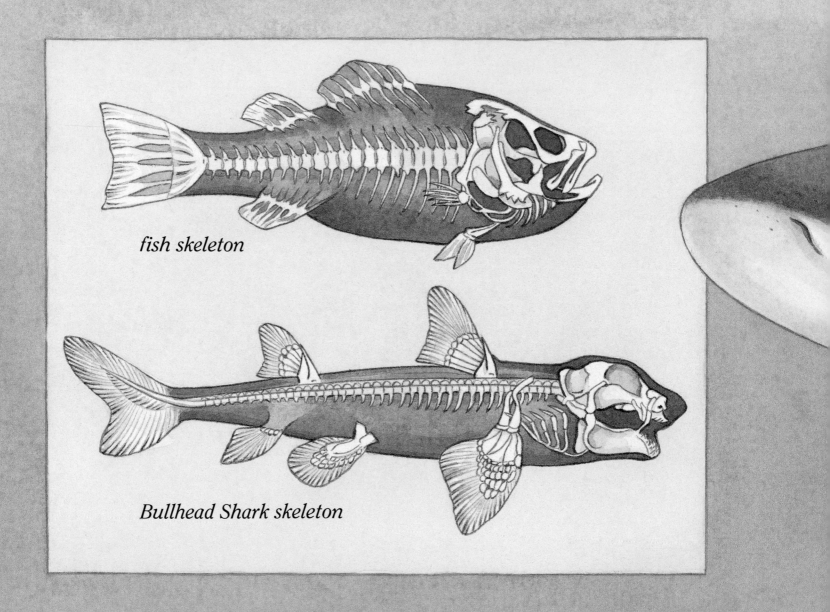

fish skeleton

Bullhead Shark skeleton

A shark's skin is rough and scratchy to the touch. It is covered with tiny sharp points called *denticles*, which means "tooth skin." As a shark grows, its old denticles drop off and are replaced by new, bigger denticles.

close-up of denticles

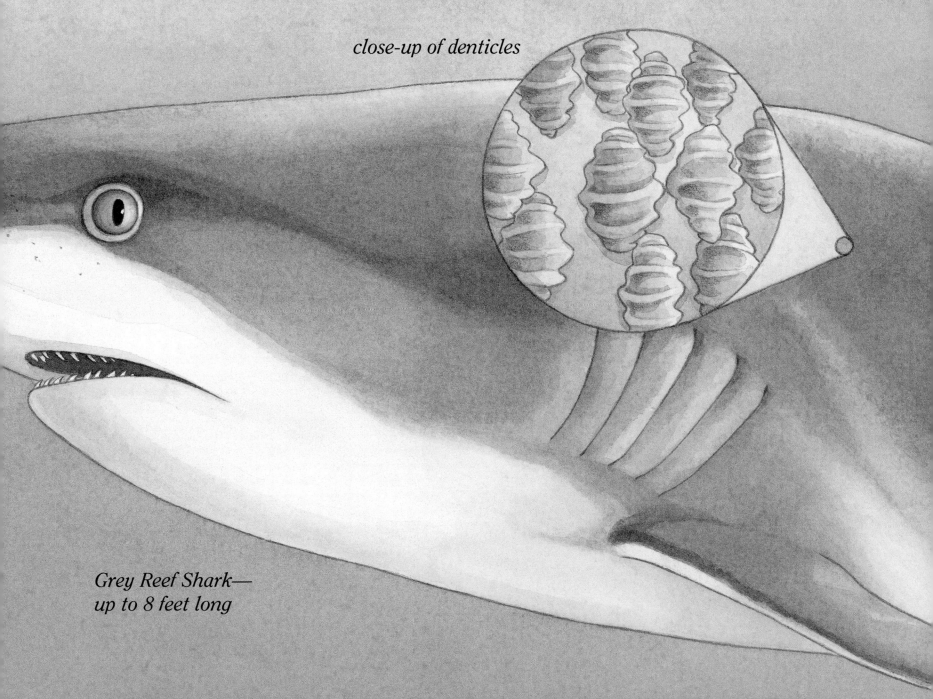

Grey Reef Shark—
up to 8 feet long

Just behind a shark's head are openings called *gill slits*. As a shark swims, water flows into its mouth and then out through the gill slits. Blood vessels in the gills take oxygen from the water.

Most kinds of sharks must keep swimming day and night to get the oxygen they need to live.

Great White Shark—up to 21 feet long

Nurse Shark—up to 14 feet long

Sharks swim by swinging their tails from side to side. The thresher shark stuns its prey with its tail fin, which is as long as its body.

A shark's other fins help it steer, keep its balance, and keep itself from sinking. When a shark swims along just below the surface of the water, you may see its *dorsal*, or back, fin slice through the water.

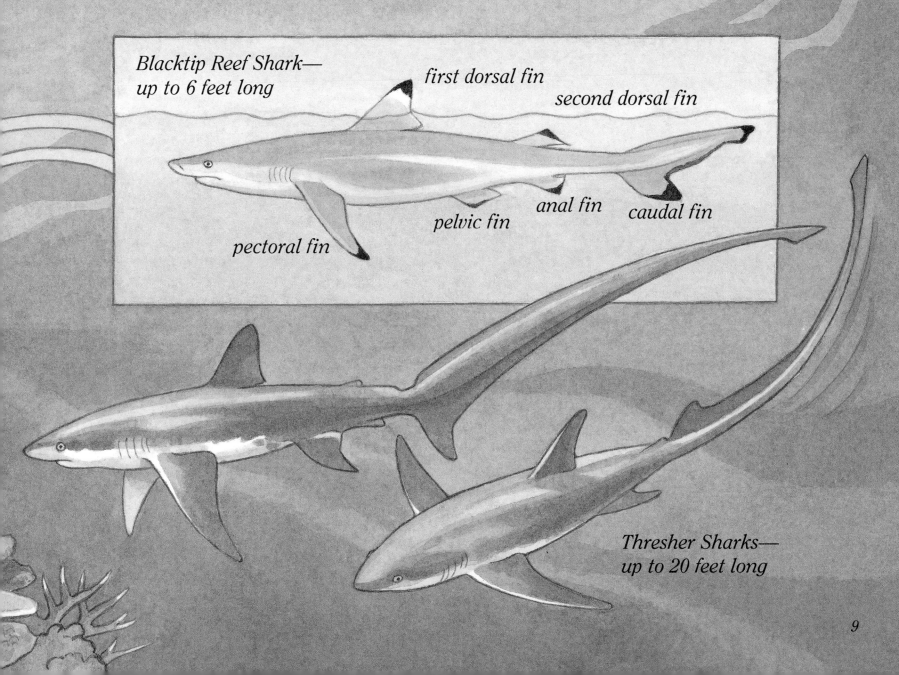

Blacktip Reef Shark—
up to 6 feet long

first dorsal fin

second dorsal fin

pelvic fin

anal fin

caudal fin

pectoral fin

Thresher Sharks—
up to 20 feet long

9

*Mako Shark—
up to 13 feet long*

Most sharks eat meat. They have many, many sharp teeth arranged in rows, one behind the other. If a front tooth is lost or broken, a new tooth quickly moves forward into its place. During its life a shark may use a thousand teeth.

The teeth of many sharks have sharp points to hold their prey and jagged edges to cut it. The horn shark has strong, flat teeth that crush the shells of the crabs it grabs.

California Horn Shark—
up to 3 feet long

Basking Shark—
up to 33 feet long

12

The biggest sharks in the oceans are gentle creatures with tiny teeth. The whale shark, basking shark, and the smaller megamouth shark all eat small animals and plants called *plankton*. The sharks swim along with their huge mouths open. All of the drifting plankton is engulfed, filtered from the water, and swallowed.

A whale shark can grow to be as long as two buses. It is the world's biggest fish. When it finds plankton or a school of small fish, it opens its mouth, then swings its head from side to side to suck in as many tiny creatures as it can catch.

Whale sharks are gentle giants. They will not harm people who hold onto a fin and ride along for a while.

Whale Shark—
up to 46 feet long

13

Nurse Shark—
up to 14 feet long

lateral line of sensitive
nerve cells

Sharks have keen senses that help them find food. They see very
well in the dim light beneath the surface of the sea. They can hear the
sounds of a fish moving hundreds of feet away. From even farther away,
sharks can smell the scent of blood from a wounded animal.

A line of sensitive nerve cells along a shark's sides helps it pick up
vibrations made by other creatures moving in the water. Little openings
inside a shark's snout contain other sensors that allow it to detect electric
signals. This may help the shark navigate, or find its way, underwater. Since
tiny electric charges are given off by animals' bodies, this sense also helps a
shark find food. It can sense electric charges from the heartbeat of a fish
hidden in the sand.

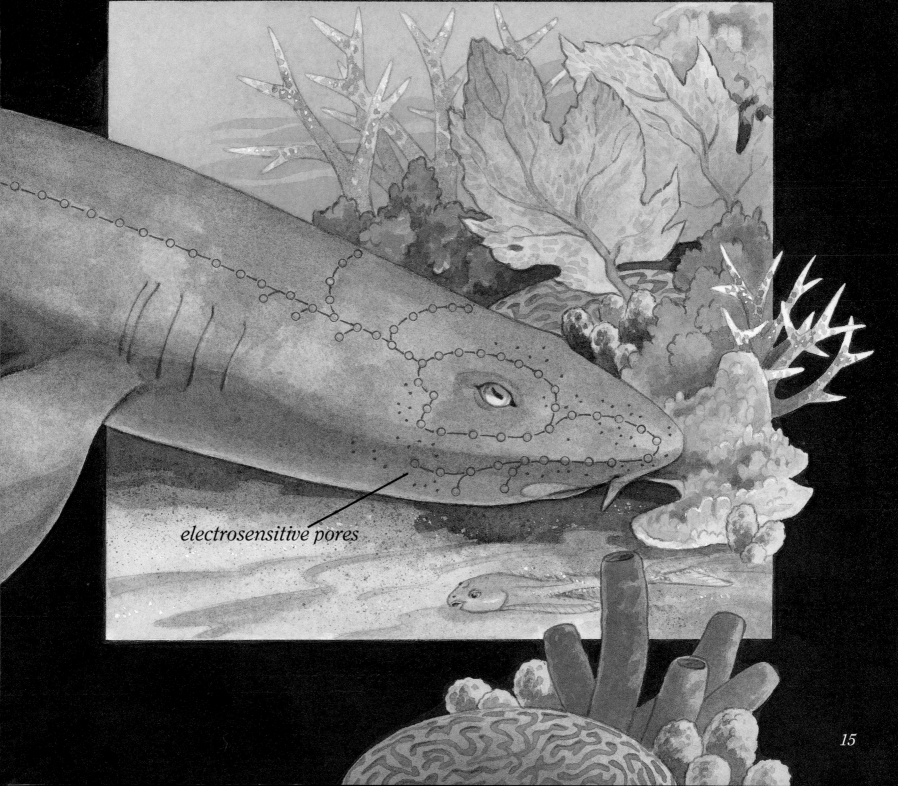

electrosensitive pores

Megalodon—probably up
to 60 feet long

Sharks first lived on Earth more than four hundred million years ago—before people, before birds, even before dinosaurs.

The open jaws of the prehistoric megalodon shark measured nearly six feet across. Like all meat-eating sharks, the megalodon shark lost many teeth. Even though megalodon sharks died out thousands of years ago, their teeth have been found on the floor of the Pacific Ocean. The teeth are usually three and half inches long.

Great White Shark—
up to 21 feet long

Megalodon tooth—
actual size

If you drew a shark, you would probably give it a long, slender body. You probably would not draw an angel shark, a swell shark, a wobbegong shark, or a cookiecutter shark.

Angel sharks have flat bodies. They usually hide on the ocean floor, ready to pounce on any fish or crab that comes near.

Swell sharks are also bottom dwellers. When a swell shark is in danger, it dives into a hideout. Then it gulps down water and swells in size so it cannot be pulled out.

Pacific Angel Shark—
up to 10 feet long

Swell Shark—
up to 3½ feet long

Wobbegong sharks also hide on the sea floor. Their colors and patterns blend in with their surroundings. Can you spot the wobbegong shark? Cookiecutters are small sharks with big sharp teeth. They take bites shaped like round cookies from the bodies of seals, whales, and dolphins.

Cookiecutter Shark—
up to 20 inches long

Ornate Wobbegong—
up to 10 feet long

19

Sometimes hundreds of scalloped hammerhead sharks gather around underwater mountain peaks called *sea mounts*. They mate in the water near the sea mounts.

There are nine different kinds of hammerhead sharks. Some are small, and some are as long as a car, but all have broad, flat heads shaped like a double-headed hammer. Their eyes look out from the tips of the hammers.

As they swim, hammerheads swing their heads from side to side. They get a good, wide view. This helps them catch fish, crabs, and squid—a favorite food.

*Scalloped Hammerheads—
up to 12 feet long*

The great white shark is the most famous—and feared—of all sharks. It is the largest meat-eating shark in the world, with the biggest teeth of all living sharks. The great white shark can swallow a whole seal in one gulp.

Great white sharks sometimes injure or kill people. These attacks on humans are rare. They usually happen when a shark mistakes a person for a food they like, especially a seal or a sea lion. Great white sharks also eat many kinds of fish, including other sharks.

Great White Shark—
up to 21 feet long

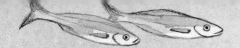

Think of all of the people who swim or dive in the oceans all over the world every year. Of all these millions of humans, only about a hundred people are bitten by sharks each year. Very few die. Besides the great white shark, several other big sharks sometimes bite people. They include grey reef sharks, oceanic whitetip sharks, and the sharks shown on these pages.

Tiger sharks are named for the striped tiger-pattern on their young. The adults eat all sorts of food, including turtles, crabs, and jellyfish. They even swallow cans and other litter in the sea.

Tiger Shark—up to 18 feet long

Mako sharks are the fastest of all sharks. They can zip along at more than thirty miles an hour and sometimes leap high out of the water.

Bull sharks sometimes leave the sea and swim far up freshwater rivers and into tropical lakes.

*Mako Shark—
up to 13 feet long*

*Bull Shark—
up to 11$\frac{1}{2}$ feet long*

People kill many millions of sharks each year. They use sharkskin to make shoes, belts, and wallets. Oil from sharks is used as an ingredient in cosmetics, including lipsticks. Shark teeth are used for jewelry.

People eat shark meat. Sometimes a shark's name is changed to make it more appealing when it is served in restaurants. The dogfish shark may be called cape shark or even rock salmon.

Soup made from shark fins is enjoyed by many people in Asia. Fisherman often cut the fins from a shark, then let it go. The shark cannot swim well and may starve to death.

People kill so many sharks that some kinds of sharks may disappear completely from the seas.

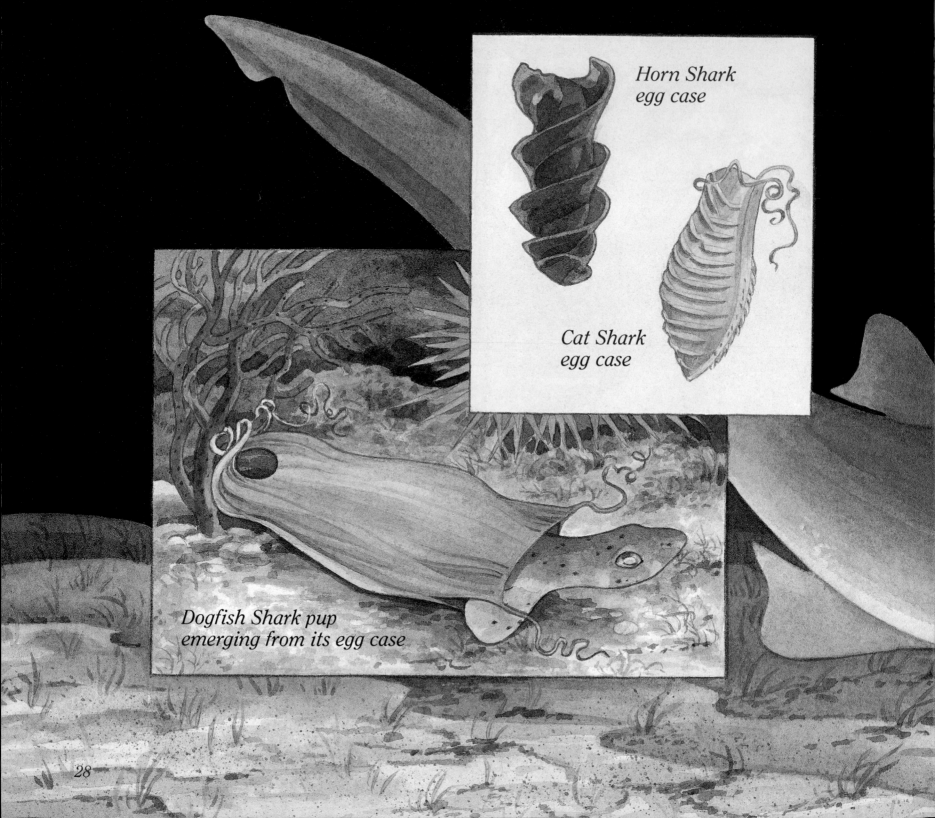

Horn Shark
egg case

Cat Shark
egg case

Dogfish Shark pup
emerging from its egg case

Even if people stop killing sharks, the population will not recover for many years. Sharks reproduce slowly, with only a few young born to a mother each year.

Some shark mothers lay eggs. They leave the eggs in a safe place; the eggs are protected by a tough, leathery case. The egg case of a dogfish shark is called a mermaid's purse. Months pass before the baby shark is ready to hatch. It is called a *pup*.

Many mother sharks give birth to live pups. Fish and other creatures try to eat shark pups, and only a few grow to be adults.

Lemon Shark giving birth

Certain kinds of fish rely on sharks. Remoras stick themselves with suckers to shark bodies. Pilot fish swim close to sharks. Both remoras and pilot fish may grab food scraps when a shark eats. Both may be safe from enemies when they are close to a shark. Remoras also help sharks by eating little creatures called *copepods* that cling to a shark's body and fins.

Sharks are an important part of ocean food chains. They eat stingrays. In places where many sharks have been killed, stingray numbers have grown. Now it seems that more and more dolphins are hurt and sometimes killed by the sharp spines of stingrays.

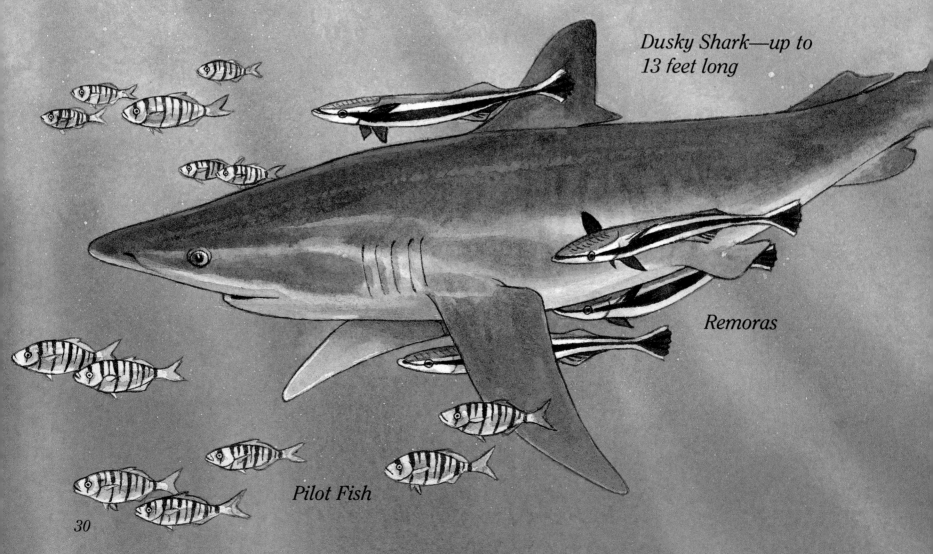

Dusky Shark—up to 13 feet long

Remoras

Pilot Fish

Oceanic Whitetip Shark—
up to 13 feet long

Sharks also eat octopuses. In places where many sharks have been killed,
octopus numbers have grown and lobsters have become scarce. Probably the
octopuses have killed most of the lobsters in those places.

People are only beginning to understand the value of sharks, but we know they are a vital part of ocean life. And we know already that the world's oceans would seem much less wild and wonderful without them.

Grey Reef Sharks— up to 8 feet long

Epaulette Shark— up to 3 1/2 feet long